This Planner Belongs To:

School Period/Year

_____

Copyright © 2022 by Naci Sigler

All rights reserved. No part of this book may be reproduced in any manner whatsoever without written permission except in the case of brief quotations embodied in critical articles and reviews.

First Printing, 2022

Table of Contents

FORWARD **5**

    Seating Chart or Classroom Layout 6

    Typical Daily Schedule 7

    Assessments -or- Grade Book 8

    Personal Planner Key Pages Index 12

    Notes 16

    Important Family Contacts 21

    Holidays and Special Days 24

    Holidays & Other Special Days 25

    Typical Daily Schedule 26

Month _____ **27**

    Monthly Calendar 27

    Monthly Prep Page 28

    Social Media Posts Scheduler 29

    Monthly Lesson Planner 31

    Monthly Expense Tracker 35

Monthly Financial Income | Tuition, Other Fees, & Donations   37

Week of _____   **39**

   Weekly Curriculum Planner   39

Daily Planners/Logs   **40**

   Daily Recurring Habits/Responsibilities   40

   Day Planners/Logs   41

   Small Groups or Lesson Focus   42

FORWARD

Hello and thank you for buying my planner! My goal is to assemble a truly complete, all-in-one teacher planner. If I missed anything, please let me know. I'll make the forms and email them to you for free as my sincere thank you gift.

You should have received two documents for downloading. This is the first and it contains all of the planner forms page numbered. The second version doesn't have page numbers. To organize these, I would suggest a binder with a set of monthly dividers. These are available from Amazon, any office supply store, or directly from us at www.relgis.store Using this method, you can easily keep the un-numbered pages organized and make as many copies as needed. For an even more organized approach, you can manually number the pages.

Respectfully,

Naci Sigler

Seating Chart or Classroom Layout

Notes: _____

_____

Typical Daily Schedule

Time & Activity	Notes
8:00	
8:30	
9:00	
9:30	
10:00	
10:30	
11:00	
11:30	
12:00	
12:30	
1:00	
1:30	
2:00	
2:30	
3:00	
3:30	
4:00	
4:30	
5:00	

Assessments -or- Grade Book

Student Name

Skill/Topic -OR- Grade

Skill/Topic -OR- Grade	Student Name				

Skill/Topic -OR- Grade

Student Name

Skill/Topic -OR- Grade	Student Name					

Personal Planner Key Pages Index

Topic	Page(s)

Topic	Page(s)

Topic	Page(s)

Topic Page(s)

NOTES

NOTES

NOTES

NOTES

NOTES

Important Family Contacts

Name	Daytime Phone #	Email

Name	Daytime Phone #	Email

Utility, Contractors, & Other Important Service Providers

Name/Company	Phone #	Account Number	Passcode

Holidays and Special Days

Date	Holiday	Day
Sept. 5, 2022	Labor Day	Monday
Sept. 11, 2022	Grandparents' Day	Sunday
Sept. 11, 2022	Patriot Day or September 11th	Sunday
Sept. 16, 2022	Stepfamily Day	Friday
Sept. 17, 2022	Citizenship Day	Saturday
Sept. 23, 2022	Native American Day	Friday
Oct. 10, 2022	Columbus Day	Monday
Oct. 15, 2022	Sweetest Day	Saturday
Oct. 17, 2022	Boss's Day	Monday
Oct. 31, 2022	Halloween	Monday
Nov. 6, 2022	Daylight Saving (End)	Sunday
Nov. 11, 2022	Veterans' Day	Friday
Nov. 24, 2022	Thanksgiving	Thursday
Nov. 25, 2022	Black Friday	Friday
Nov. 28, 2022	Cyber Monday	Monday
Dec. 7, 2022	Pearl Harbor Remembrance Day	Wednesday
Dec. 25, 2022	Christmas Day	Sunday
Dec. 31, 2022	New Year's Eve	Saturday

Date	Holiday	Day
Jan. 1, 2023	New Year's Day	Sunday
Jan. 16, 2023	Martin Luther King Day	Monday
Jan. 24, 2023	Belly Laugh Day	Tuesday
Feb. 2, 2023	Groundhog Day	Thursday
Feb. 12, 2023	Lincoln's Birthday	Sunday
Feb. 14, 2023	Valentine's Day	Tuesday
Feb. 20, 2023	Presidents Day and Washington's Birthday	Monday
Feb. 21, 2023	Mardi Gras Carnival *(New Orleans)*	Tuesday
Mar. 12, 2023	Daylight Saving *(Start)*	Sunday
Mar. 17, 2023	St. Patrick's Day	Friday
Apr. 1, 2023	April Fool's Day	Saturday
Apr. 7, 2023	Good Friday	Friday
Apr. 9, 2023	Easter	Sunday
Apr. 10, 2023	Easter Monday	Monday
Apr. 22, 2023	Earth Day	Saturday
May 5, 2023	Cinco de Mayo	Friday
May 14, 2023	Mother's Day	Sunday
May 20, 2023	Armed Forces Day	Saturday
May 28, 2023	Pentecost	Sunday
May 29, 2023	Memorial Day	Monday
May 29, 2023	Pentecost Monday	Monday

Typical Daily Schedule

Time & Activity	Notes
8:00	
8:30	
9:00	
9:30	
10:00	
10:30	
11:00	
11:30	
12:00	
12:30	
1:00	
1:30	
2:00	
2:30	
3:00	
3:30	
4:00	
4:30	
5:00	

MONTH/YEAR: _____

SUN	MON	TUE	WED	THU	FRI	SAT

PRIORITIES
- ☐ _____
- ☐ _____
- ☐ _____
- ☐ _____

NOTES _____

_____

_____

_____

_____

MONTHLY PREP PAGE

As the month begins, don't forget to...

Personal To-Do

Work To-Do

Shopping List

Social Media Posts Scheduler

* Tip: Fill in the Holidays and Special Day's like Grandparents' Day first. Then, you can fill in special day projects.
* Don't forget to take pics!

1	
2	
3	
4	
5	
6	
7	
8	
9	
10	
11	
12	
13	
14	

15	
16	
17	
18	
19	
20	
21	
22	
23	
24	
25	
26	
27	
28	
29	
30	
31	

Monthly Lesson Planner

Monthly Expense Tracker

Date	Description	Amount, Check for Auto Pay

Date	Description	Amount, Check for Auto Pay

Monthly Financial Income | Tuition, Other Fees, & Donations

Date	Payer/Description	Amount

Date	Payer/Description	Amount

Weekly Curriculum Planner

Monday	
Tuesday	
Wednesday	
Thursday	
Friday	
Saturday	
Sunday	

Daily Recurring Habits/Responsibilities

NOTES

Week of:

Day Planner

Time & Activity	Notes
8:00	
8:30	
9:00	
9:30	
10:00	
10:30	
11:00	
11:30	
12:00	
12:30	
1:00	
1:30	
2:00	
2:30	
3:00	
3:30	
4:00	
4:30	
5:00	

Small Groups or Lesson Focus

Group Members	
**Focus Skills	Objectives**	
Lesson Title/Name	
Materials	
Notes	

* If you don't need to write the group members each time, you can just skip that box. You could assign them to groups named by color (avoid red, black, brown), flowers, etc. If anyone has to change groups, make a note on this page.

Day Planner

Time & Activity	Notes
8:00	
8:30	
9:00	
9:30	
10:00	
10:30	
11:00	
11:30	
12:00	
12:30	
1:00	
1:30	
2:00	
2:30	
3:00	
3:30	
4:00	
4:30	
5:00	

Small Groups or Lesson Focus

Group Members	
Focus Skills | Objectives	
Lesson Title/Name	
Materials	
Notes	

Day Planner

Time & Activity	Notes
8:00	
8:30	
9:00	
9:30	
10:00	
10:30	
11:00	
11:30	
12:00	
12:30	
1:00	
1:30	
2:00	
2:30	
3:00	
3:30	
4:00	
4:30	
5:00	

Small Groups or Lesson Focus

Group Members	
Focus Skills | Objectives	
Lesson Title/Name	
Materials	
Notes	

Day Planner

Time & Activity	Notes
8:00	
8:30	
9:00	
9:30	
10:00	
10:30	
11:00	
11:30	
12:00	
12:30	
1:00	
1:30	
2:00	
2:30	
3:00	
3:30	
4:00	
4:30	
5:00	

Small Groups or Lesson Focus

Group Members	
Focus Skills | Objectives	
Lesson Title/Name	
Materials	
Notes	

Day Planner

Time & Activity	Notes
8:00	
8:30	
9:00	
9:30	
10:00	
10:30	
11:00	
11:30	
12:00	
12:30	
1:00	
1:30	
2:00	
2:30	
3:00	
3:30	
4:00	
4:30	
5:00	

Small Groups or Lesson Focus

Group Members	
Focus Skills | Objectives	
Lesson Title/Name	
Materials	
Notes	

Day Planner

Time & Activity	Notes
8:00	
8:30	
9:00	
9:30	
10:00	
10:30	
11:00	
11:30	
12:00	
12:30	
1:00	
1:30	
2:00	
2:30	
3:00	
3:30	
4:00	
4:30	
5:00	

Small Groups or Lesson Focus

Group Members	
Focus Skills | Objectives	
Lesson Title/Name	
Materials	
Notes	

Day Planner

Time & Activity	Notes
8:00	
8:30	
9:00	
9:30	
10:00	
10:30	
11:00	
11:30	
12:00	
12:30	
1:00	
1:30	
2:00	
2:30	
3:00	
3:30	
4:00	
4:30	
5:00	

Small Groups or Lesson Focus

Group Members	
Focus Skills | Objectives	
Lesson Title/Name	
Materials	
Notes	

End of the Week Reflection

NOTES

This Planner Belongs To:

School Period/Year

_____

Copyright © 2022 by Naci Sigler

All rights reserved. No part of this book may be reproduced in any manner whatsoever without written permission except in the case of brief quotations embodied in critical articles and reviews.

First Printing, 2022

Table of Contents

FORWARD   5

    Seating Chart or Classroom Layout   6

    Typical Daily Schedule   7

    Assessments -or- Grade Book   8

    Personal Planner Key Pages Index   12

    Notes   16

    Important Family Contacts   21

    Holidays and Special Days   24

    Holidays & Other Special Days   25

    Typical Daily Schedule   26

Month _____   27

    Monthly Calendar   27

    Monthly Prep Page   28

    Social Media Posts Scheduler   29

    Monthly Lesson Planner   31

    Monthly Expense Tracker   35

Monthly Financial Income | Tuition, Other Fees, & Donations   37

Week of _____   39

   Weekly Curriculum Planner   39

Daily Planners/Logs   40

   Daily Recurring Habits/Responsibilities   40
   Day Planners/Logs   41
   Small Groups or Lesson Focus   42

FORWARD

Hello and thank you for buying my planner! My goal is to assemble a truly complete, all-in-one teacher planner. If I missed anything, please let me know. I'll make the forms and email them to you for free as my sincere thank you gift.

You should have received two documents for downloading. This is the first and it contains all of the planner forms page numbered. The second version doesn't have page numbers. To organize these, I would suggest a binder with a set of monthly dividers. These are available from Amazon, any office supply store, or directly from us at www.relgis.store Using this method, you can easily keep the un-numbered pages organized and make as many copies as needed. For an even more organized approach, you can manually number the pages.

Respectfully,

Naci Sigler

Seating Chart or Classroom Layout

Notes:

Typical Daily Schedule

Time & Activity	Notes
8:00	
8:30	
9:00	
9:30	
10:00	
10:30	
11:00	
11:30	
12:00	
12:30	
1:00	
1:30	
2:00	
2:30	
3:00	
3:30	
4:00	
4:30	
5:00	

Assessments -or- Grade Book

Student Name

Skill/Topic -OR- Grade

Skill/Topic -OR- Grade

Student Name

Skill/Topic -OR- Grade	Student Name				

Skill/Topic -OR- Grade	**Student Name**				

Personal Planner Key Pages Index

Topic	Page(s)

Topic **Page(s)**

Topic | **Page(s)**

Topic **Page(s)**

NOTES

NOTES

NOTES

NOTES

NOTES

Important Family Contacts

Name	Daytime Phone #	Email

Name	Daytime Phone #	Email

Utility, Contractors, & Other Important Service Providers

Name/Company	Phone #	Account Number	Passcode

Holidays and Special Days

Date	Holiday	Day
Sept. 5, 2022	Labor Day	Monday
Sept. 11, 2022	Grandparents' Day	Sunday
Sept. 11, 2022	Patriot Day or September 11th	Sunday
Sept. 16, 2022	Stepfamily Day	Friday
Sept. 17, 2022	Citizenship Day	Saturday
Sept. 23, 2022	Native American Day	Friday
Oct. 10, 2022	Columbus Day	Monday
Oct. 15, 2022	Sweetest Day	Saturday
Oct. 17, 2022	Boss's Day	Monday
Oct. 31, 2022	Halloween	Monday
Nov. 6, 2022	Daylight Saving *(End)*	Sunday
Nov. 11, 2022	Veterans' Day	Friday
Nov. 24, 2022	Thanksgiving	Thursday
Nov. 25, 2022	Black Friday	Friday
Nov. 28, 2022	Cyber Monday	Monday
Dec. 7, 2022	Pearl Harbor Remembrance Day	Wednesday
Dec. 25, 2022	Christmas Day	Sunday
Dec. 31, 2022	New Year's Eve	Saturday

Date	Holiday	Day
Jan. 1, 2023	New Year's Day	Sunday
Jan. 16, 2023	Martin Luther King Day	Monday
Jan. 24, 2023	Belly Laugh Day	Tuesday
Feb. 2, 2023	Groundhog Day	Thursday
Feb. 12, 2023	Lincoln's Birthday	Sunday
Feb. 14, 2023	Valentine's Day	Tuesday
Feb. 20, 2023	Presidents Day and Washington's Birthday	Monday
Feb. 21, 2023	Mardi Gras Carnival *(New Orleans)*	Tuesday
Mar. 12, 2023	Daylight Saving *(Start)*	Sunday
Mar. 17, 2023	St. Patrick's Day	Friday
Apr. 1, 2023	April Fool's Day	Saturday
Apr. 7, 2023	Good Friday	Friday
Apr. 9, 2023	Easter	Sunday
Apr. 10, 2023	Easter Monday	Monday
Apr. 22, 2023	Earth Day	Saturday
May 5, 2023	Cinco de Mayo	Friday
May 14, 2023	Mother's Day	Sunday
May 20, 2023	Armed Forces Day	Saturday
May 28, 2023	Pentecost	Sunday
May 29, 2023	Memorial Day	Monday
May 29, 2023	Pentecost Monday	Monday

Typical Daily Schedule

Time & Activity	Notes
8:00	
8:30	
9:00	
9:30	
10:00	
10:30	
11:00	
11:30	
12:00	
12:30	
1:00	
1:30	
2:00	
2:30	
3:00	
3:30	
4:00	
4:30	
5:00	

MONTH/YEAR: _____

SUN	MON	TUE	WED	THU	FRI	SAT

PRIORITIES
- ☐ _____
- ☐ _____
- ☐ _____
- ☐ _____

NOTES _____

_____

_____

_____

_____

MONTHLY PREP PAGE

As the month begins, don't forget to...

Personal To-Do

Work To-Do

Shopping List

Social Media Posts Scheduler

* Tip: Fill in the Holidays and Special Day's like Grandparents' Day first. Then, you can fill in special day projects.
* Don't forget to take pics!

1	
2	
3	
4	
5	
6	
7	
8	
9	
10	
11	
12	
13	
14	

15	
16	
17	
18	
19	
20	
21	
22	
23	
24	
25	
26	
27	
28	
29	
30	
31	

Monthly Lesson Planner

Monthly Expense Tracker

Date	Description	Amount, Check for Auto Pay

Date	Description	Amount, Check for Auto Pay

Monthly Financial Income | Tuition, Other Fees, & Donations

Date	Payer/Description	Amount

Date	Payer/Description	Amount

Weekly Curriculum Planner

Monday	
Tuesday	
Wednesday	
Thursday	
Friday	
Saturday	
Sunday	

Daily Recurring Habits/Responsibilities

NOTES

Week of:

Day Planner

Time & Activity	Notes
8:00	
8:30	
9:00	
9:30	
10:00	
10:30	
11:00	
11:30	
12:00	
12:30	
1:00	
1:30	
2:00	
2:30	
3:00	
3:30	
4:00	
4:30	
5:00	

Small Groups or Lesson Focus

Group Members	
Focus Skills | Objectives	
Lesson Title/Name	
Materials	
Notes	

* If you don't need to write the group members each time, you can just skip that box. You could assign them to groups named by color (avoid red, black, brown), flowers, etc. If anyone has to change groups, make a note on this page.

Day Planner

Time & Activity	Notes
8:00	
8:30	
9:00	
9:30	
10:00	
10:30	
11:00	
11:30	
12:00	
12:30	
1:00	
1:30	
2:00	
2:30	
3:00	
3:30	
4:00	
4:30	
5:00	

Small Groups or Lesson Focus

Group Members	
**Focus Skills	Objectives**	
Lesson Title/Name	
Materials	
Notes	

Day Planner

Time & Activity	Notes
8:00	
8:30	
9:00	
9:30	
10:00	
10:30	
11:00	
11:30	
12:00	
12:30	
1:00	
1:30	
2:00	
2:30	
3:00	
3:30	
4:00	
4:30	
5:00	

Small Groups or Lesson Focus

Group Members	
Focus Skills | Objectives	
Lesson Title/Name	
Materials	
Notes	

Day Planner

Time & Activity	Notes
8:00	
8:30	
9:00	
9:30	
10:00	
10:30	
11:00	
11:30	
12:00	
12:30	
1:00	
1:30	
2:00	
2:30	
3:00	
3:30	
4:00	
4:30	
5:00	

Small Groups or Lesson Focus

Group Members	
Focus Skills | Objectives	
Lesson Title/Name	
Materials	
Notes	

Day Planner

Time & Activity	Notes
8:00	
8:30	
9:00	
9:30	
10:00	
10:30	
11:00	
11:30	
12:00	
12:30	
1:00	
1:30	
2:00	
2:30	
3:00	
3:30	
4:00	
4:30	
5:00	

Small Groups or Lesson Focus

Group Members	
**Focus Skills	Objectives**	
Lesson Title/Name	
Materials	
Notes	

Day Planner

Time & Activity	Notes
8:00	
8:30	
9:00	
9:30	
10:00	
10:30	
11:00	
11:30	
12:00	
12:30	
1:00	
1:30	
2:00	
2:30	
3:00	
3:30	
4:00	
4:30	
5:00	

Small Groups or Lesson Focus

Group Members	
Focus Skills | Objectives	
Lesson Title/Name	
Materials	
Notes	

Day Planner

Time & Activity		Notes
8:00		
8:30		
9:00		
9:30		
10:00		
10:30		
11:00		
11:30		
12:00		
12:30		
1:00		
1:30		
2:00		
2:30		
3:00		
3:30		
4:00		
4:30		
5:00		

Small Groups or Lesson Focus

Group Members	
Focus Skills | Objectives	
Lesson Title/Name	
Materials	
Notes	

End of the Week Reflection

NOTES